GURUS

R. D. CLEMENTS

INTER-VARSITY PRESS
DOWNERS GROVE
ILLINOIS 60515

InterVarsity Press is the book
publishing division of Inter-Varsity
Christian Fellowship, a student
movement active on campus at
hundreds of universities,
colleges and schools of nursing. For
information about Inter-Varsity
Christian Fellowship, write IVCF, 233
Langdon, Madison, WI 53703.

ISBN 0-87784-449-6

Printed in the United States of America

CONTENTS

1   BASIC EASTERN THOUGHT   7

2   THE DIVINE LIGHT MISSION   17

3   THE HARE KRISHNA MOVEMENT (ISKCON)   25

4   TRANSCENDENTAL MEDITATION   30

5   MYSTICISM: A CHRISTIAN CRITIQUE   35

6   THE CHALLENGE OF EASTERN THOUGHT   44

APPENDIX: PRACTICAL ADVICE TO CHRISTIANS
DEALING WITH EASTERN MYSTIC GROUPS   57

INTRODUCTION

Dancing figures chant the names of Hindu gods in O'Hare Airport in Chicago; guileless, tranquil gurus smile beneficently down from billboards upon scurrying, busy, London officeworkers; the East has come West. Christians, whose major foe in recent times has been materialism, have suddenly to confront an alternative philosophy which is quite blatantly *spiritual* in emphasis. Some are profoundly taken aback by the prolific success of Eastern sects, particularly among the young. Surely, they say, India is a country of heathen superstition and idolatry; what possible appeal can such a culture hold for modern Western society?

The present interest in Eastern mysticism should not, in fact, be such a great surprise. It is just a part of a much more general trend in thinking, the characteristic features of which we can easily identify.

SUSPICION OF DOGMA The need for international understanding in a nuclear age and the loss of any sense of absolute authority in the realm of religious truth and morality have combined to make "intolerance" the unforgivable sin of the twentieth century. Eastern religions generally, and Hinduism in particular, are able in a quite remarkable way to absorb practically any other religion and reinterpret it into Eastern terms. They seem, therefore, to be the ideal jumping-off point in the search for a philosophy to unite a divided world.

DISILLUSION WITH RATIONALISM The characteristic philosophy of our age is existentialist. This is basically a reaction against the extremes of scientific rationalism which, many feel, tend to dehumanize man to the level of a biochemical machine. The great emphasis on experience, irrationality and absurdity among avant-garde elements in the art world in the West is further evidence of this reaction against reason. In every Eastern religion experience is of central importance. Indeed, many varieties of Hindu and Buddhist practice are just different methods of achieving the ultimate experience of enlightenment. Furthermore, Eastern thought is antagonistic at its root to the methodology of scientific inquiry and to the knowledge gained thereby. Hinduism also inculcates a far greater respect for animal life than is common in the West, where many fear that technology has exploited creation almost to the point of self-destruction. In every way, the East has preserved values which a science-dominated West has abandoned. So it was inevitable that the existentialist reaction be accompanied by a revival of interest in mysticism.

DISILLUSION WITH MATERIALISM Christianity has always insisted that material benefits alone are inadequate to satisfy man's need. Many young people have discovered the truth of that. In recent years we have seen beatniks, flower people, hippies, etc., all expressing the same rejection of materialistic values. Unfortunately, the Christian church seems as acquisitive as everybody else. In the East, however, it is possible to find not only a religion that emphasizes the need to discover internal contentment independent of material things, but also living examples of ascetics who have renounced worldly possessions to achieve that contentment. Whereas Christianity seems to be generally compromised and corrupted with hypocrisy, the East offers a pristine genuineness and simplicity as well as a certain novelty to Western young people.

The success of mystic sects recently, then, is no mere flash in the pan. It is quite likely that the whole of Western culture may become increasingly influenced by Eastern ideas. The popularity of a book like *Jonathan Livingston Seagull*[1] witnesses to this. My aim in this present book is to help Christians to understand Eastern sects, and particularly the three which are best known: the Divine Light Mission, the International Society for Krishna Consciousness and Transcendental Meditation. There are insights in these groups which Christians must rediscover and also serious errors which they must vigorously combat. In attempting to assess and point out these matters, this book is unashamedly prejudiced toward the Christian faith. Nevertheless, it is to be hoped that those who are interested in mysticism will find this Christian critique both fair and challenging.

BASIC EASTERN THOUGHT

1

The problem of understanding Eastern thought is not merely one of grasping new concepts, but of appreciating a basically different epistemology (theory of knowledge). Western thinking has been dominated by scientific ideas of what it means to know something. A fundamental principle in this is analysis and classification through the use of reason. We understand a thing by splitting it up, somehow, into parts or causes, and then we give names to each item of our analysis so that our knowledge is verbally communicable. We do not feel we really know something until we can represent it to ourselves as a linear progression of simple ideas (that is, "words") in this analytical way. Basic to the whole process is the separation of ourselves as subject (the knower) from the thing we are investigating as object (the known).

An important feature of Eastern thinking, however, is its general rejection of scientific knowledge of this type. Indian and Taoist philosophy sees reality as "non-dual," that is, not divided. The world of conventional knowledge which distinguishes "the many" by divisions, analyses and words is regarded as *maya* (illusion). The basic quest, for Eastern religion, is to find release (*moksha*) from this diversity and to experience the essential oneness of the universe with oneself (*samadhi*). In its very nature, this experience cannot be described or analyzed in words, but one may arrive at it by various paths. This becomes clearer when we see how this basic philosophy (*monism*) influences the Eastern concepts of some typical Christian doctrines.

CREATION In Genesis 1, God gives names to his creation: "Heaven" (v. 8), "Earth" and "Seas" (v. 10). He also pronounces an objective valuation of his work: "It was good." These things are important because they show us that the God of the Bible is in no sense to be identified with his creation. He possesses a distinct, personal existence over against the created world. He is the "I am" (Ex. 3:14), a title indicating both independent existence and self-consciousness.

All this is in severe contrast to Eastern thought. The idea of a God who self-consciously discriminates among creation with words or names is a complete capitulation to the maya. Rather, Brahman (the essential unitary reality, the "god," of the universe) *grows* into the universe, manifesting itself in diversity by way of a divine "prank" or "play" (*lila*). There is no decision or purpose in Brahman since the whole idea of self-consciousness is foreign to it.

TIME The dismemberment of the one into the many continues forever in eras of one *kalpa* each in length (4,320,000,000 years). Within these great periods some Hindu groups see significance in astrological ages. Due to the precession of the equinoxes, the signs of the zodiac are not perfectly stationary relative to the solar year. From about A.D. 200-2300 is the age of Pisces the Fish, which some link with the dominance of Christianity. Around A.D. 2300, however, we move into the age of Aquarius, thought by many to signal a time of great peace and harmony. Thus, for Eastern philosophy generally, time is cyclic.

In biblical thought, however, time, which is part of the created order, is finite and linear. It progresses from creation, the beginning (Greek *archē*), to an end goal (Greek *telos*) with a definite purpose. This is because the Creator is personal, transcendent, non-capricious and has a plan (Eph. 3:11).

SIN In Genesis 1 and 2, God makes man "in his own image" as a self-conscious, personal being who possesses limited sovereignty over creation (1:27-28). In token of this, he brings to man representatives of the animate world which is to be his domain, so that he might name them (2:19-20). Thus man defines his "individual ego" as distinct from the rest of creation. He stands as subject over against the rest of the world as object, in the same way as God stands over against the entire creation. Man lost the privilege of intimate, personal fellowship with God because of moral disobedience, and that alienation continues until man's sin is forgiven and he is reconciled again to God (2 Cor. 5:19). Every man has only one life to live, and at the end of time he will be judged by the personal God who made him (Acts 17:31; Heb. 9:27).

In Eastern thought, however, man is just a part of the oneness of the universal soul (*atman*). He cannot be alienated from that oneness by moral disobedience, since it is a oneness of essence, not just of interpersonal relationship. The Brahman-atman is not a personal transcendent being and is therefore incapable of being offended. Sin, for the Eastern thinker, is essentially the *ignorance* that prevents a man from realizing his oneness with everything else. It is the root of all discontent, for discontent is derived from the desire to grasp and to hold on to things, be they material possessions or intellectual ideas or personal friendships. All such graspings lead inevitably to frustration. This can be overcome only by attaining enlightenment. Failure to achieve such release condemns man to a continual process of rebirth into other forms of life (*samsara*).

SALVATION Salvation, for an Eastern thinker, is the experience of the "oneness" of himself with all things. This is enlightenment (various Hindu and Buddhist terms are used for this experience, for example, *moksha, samadhi, satchitanand, satori*). Such an experience cannot be verbalized; one can only enter into it. But it is not far from any man since through his innermost soul he shares in that essential oneness which underlies the external universe. Salvation is thus a matter of realizing what we are, rather than of becoming what we should be. The word *realizing*, though, should not lead us to conceive of this enlightenment as a self-conscious piece of subject-object cognition. Rather, by its very nature, it requires the loss of the personal ego-consciousness of the one who is experiencing it. Hence the famous statement of an enlightened one, "I am Buddha" or "I am Brahman."

All the complexities of Eastern religion derive from the many different methods of attaining this mystical experience where self-consciousness merges into cosmic-consciousness. The Hindu term for these different roads to enlightenment or union is *yoga*. Perhaps the best known types of yoga are those that involve *meditative* discipline, but there are many others. In fact, some branch of Eastern religion has turned practically every sort of human activity into a yoga that leads to enlightenment. For the intellectual gymnast there are *jnana yoga* and the subtleties of Zen Buddhism. Good works are given a place in *karma yoga,* although it is important to understand that the moral effort involved in this discipline is motivated by expediency, not by genuine altruism. Good *karma* takes a person nearer enlightenment; bad *karma* results in a step down in the next incarnation. For the religious ritualist there is *krija yoga*. Even the act of copulation has been turned into a yoga discipline—*tantric yoga*. But perhaps the most significant pathway to enlightenment in the recent Western movements is *bhakti yoga*. This involves religious devotion and service to a spiritual master. It is the nearest Eastern thought gets to a *personal* relationship with "god." All, however, have in common the idea that a man finds his own salvation through personal discipline and effort, and that this enlightenment has nothing to do with *moral* issues.

The situation for the Christian is quite different. The Bible teaches that man stands in need of salvation primarily from his moral failure, and only secondarily from his ignorance of God. This, though real, is nevertheless only a product of this moral alienation. A man can know God personally when his moral sinfulness has been dealt with. It is the Christian belief that in Jesus Christ God has provided a means for the forgiveness of man's sins, since man was morally impotent to save himself.

JESUS CHRIST The Bible teaches that Jesus was absolutely unique. The whole of Old Testament history pointed forward to him, and the church he founded must look back to him continually in the communion supper he inaugurated (Lk. 24:44-47; 1 Cor. 11:23-26). This was because he came not only to teach, but to accomplish salvation for men by means of his death on the cross and his resurrection (Lk. 19:10; Rom. 5:8). The Bible makes it clear that, though he was perfect man, he was also the eternal, personal self-expression of the Godhead (Jn. 1:1; Col. 1:15). The mystery of the Trinity reveals that within God there is a complex of three self-conscious persons, and Jesus was the incarnation of the second of those persons—God's Son. That he should be perfect God and perfect man was necessary if he was to accomplish salvation for sinful men (Heb. 7:15-28). Furthermore, his coming to be man's savior was part of the eternal purpose which God had when he created the world (Eph. 3:11; 1 Pet. 1:20).

Now the Eastern religions give considerable attention to the appearance of incarnations of "god" in history, though these are by no means essential to the underlying monistic philosophy we have already outlined. Rather, it is that certain types of Hinduism (using bhakti yoga) and one particular branch of Buddhism (*Mahayana*) have as a central element in their pathway to enlightenment devotion to an *avatar*, that is, a personal incarnation of "god." It is a common belief that through the grace of one of these avatars an individual can be granted enlightenment. These incarnations do not accomplish anything to secure salvation, but while they are in the world the faithful disciple may seek the experience of enlightenment from them. They act as transmitters of the enlightenment experience, not as saviors who make redemption possible. They are not unique, though it seems to be generally believed that there can be only one true incarnation at any particular time.

THE SCRIPTURES By the very nature of Brahman-atman it is clear that Eastern religion excludes the idea of a verbal revelation of God. God can only be experienced, and the scriptures can only describe the ways in which this experience can be sought. Nevertheless, the *Vedic* literature of Hinduism is enormous enough to daunt all but the most determined reader. In addition to this canonical literature (the *Vedas*), however, there is a large body of further commentary on the Vedas, usually called the *Vedantic* literature. Much of this relates to the personal incarnations of Brahman and to Bhakti devotion to these incarnations as a way to enlightenment. One of the most influential books in this field is the Bhagavad Gita, which relates the stories of Krishna (an incarnation) and where the idea of love for "god" finds clear expression.

In contrast, the Bible clearly regards itself as the verbal revelation of the personal transcendent God who is able to speak as subject to man as object. It is the authoritative record and interpreter of the saving and revealing acts of God in history, and as such makes propositional statements about the character and purpose of God which are true, though the finiteness of the human intellect may require that God sometimes accommodates what he says about himself to our limited understanding. A man may be a Hindu and even attain enlightenment with no intellectual knowledge of the Vedas. But to be a Christian a man must know something about God and about the way of salvation, and ultimately this must come from the Bible.

PRAYER AND MEDITATION Jesus taught his disciples to pray using words that clearly reflect an interpersonal I-thou relationship between God and man (Mt. 6:9-13). The Christian must address God ("Our Father") as one who is separate and distinct from him ("who art in heaven"). Even in those instances where mystical experiences of some kind are described in Scripture (Is. 6; Ezek. 1; Rev. 1), there is no idea of merging with God. Rather this I-thou distinction is heightened (for example, Is. 6:5) and is accompanied by a sense of personal moral failure. Where the Bible speaks of "meditating," it is always in context of deeply considering the law of God (for example, Ps. 1:2; 119:15, 97) or the works of God (Ps. 77:12). It is meditation *on* God, in the light of all he has been to us (Ps. 63:5-8), and therefore never without definite cognitive content. Some Christians (mainly in the Catholic tradition) have practised meditation of the mind-emptying variety (for example, St. John of the Cross), but there seems to be no biblical warrant for such a practice. Neither is there any clear biblical method of interpreting the experiences obtained in this way. According to the Bible it is *prayer* rather than meditation which is the normative Christian practice. The idea of an I-thou relationship with the distinct, personal Creator- and Redeemer-God is always central.

Now some Buddhist and Hindu devotion involves prayers to a particular incarnation, but this is always seen as a means toward enlightenment through the grace of the avatar, and not as real, interpersonal dialogue with "god" in any sense. The normative Eastern mystical practice, however, is meditation. Here the lack of any I-thou relationship with a personal God is clearly evident. The aim of Eastern meditation is not to meditate *on* "god's" person, but to meditate *into* his essence. By this mental discipline, the sense of ego-consciousness or individual selfhood is purged out and the meditator experiences a merging with the oneness behind the universe where all personality distinctions are obliterated.

There has been a growing interest in meditation and Eastern philosophy in the West for some time, generally amongst intellectuals. Zen Buddhism has been publicized and encouraged by writers like Alan Watts and Christmas Humphreys. During the last century a number of mystic sects established themselves, like the Ramakrishna movement and Theosophy, both of which began around 1860. Aldous Huxley was influenced considerably by such groups. In very recent times, however, there has been a great acceleration in the growth of this interest. No longer is it only an intellectual elite who are embracing these ideas. It seems increasingly likely that our whole culture may swing Eastwards in its underlying presuppositions about life. The most dramatic indication of this trend has been the phenomenal success of a number of Hindu sects and organizations. The best known are the Divine Light Mission, the Hare Krishna movement and Transcendental Meditation. We shall turn now to examine briefly the history and distinctive features of these three groups.

THE DIVINE LIGHT MISSION

The Divine Light Mission is a Vedantist Hindu movement of a Westernized type centered on devotion to the Guru Maharaj Ji, who it is claimed, is an incarnation of "god" and able to give enlightenment to his disciples.

HISTORY Shri Hans Maharaj Ji, the present Guru's father, began spreading the basic ideas of DLM in the 1920s in north India and West Pakistan. He claimed to have reached enlightenment himself by meditating on the knowledge given to him by a guru, Shri Sarupanand Ji. His first disciples were made in Delhi at a cloth mill. He seems to have been a clever and forthright man who propagated his message in the early days quite bravely and through much personal hardship. There also seems to have been in his teaching some perceptive insight into the barrenness of traditional Hindu ritualism and caste prejudice. Certainly he and his followers suffered considerable opposition, and still do, from more orthodox Hindu sects. By 1966, when he died, his disciples were numbered in millions, and the organization known as the Divine Light Mission, which he founded in 1960, was efficiently coordinating the activities of a large staff of mahatmas whose task was to spread the knowledge.

Shri Maharaj Ji was married and his wife, Mata Ji, is still alive. He has four sons, all of whom play an active part in the Mission today. The eldest brother, Bal Bhagwan Ji, is a most able exponent of some of the more difficult intellectual concepts of Vedantist Hinduism. The next two brothers, Shri Raja Ji and Shri Bhole Ji, seem to tour together occasionally. Bhole is renowned for his interest in music, particularly rock. It is in the fourth son, however, that the major interest lies—Shri Sant Ji (usually called Guru Maharaj Ji, though this is really a title rather than a name). It is claimed that all the members of the family are fully realized avatars who in normal times would each be *Satguru* (Perfect Master). But in this specially favored time at the end of *kaliyuga* (the age of darkness), there has been a particularly powerful manifestation of "god." These other avatars have been manifested only in a serving capacity to the true guru for this age, that is, Maharaj Ji, who was born in 1958.

The claim of this fourth son to be the supreme manifestation of "god" was recognized at the funeral of his father, when the boy (then aged eight) said to the weeping devotees, "Oh, you have been deluded by the maya;

Maharaj Ji is here, very much present among you. Recognize him, adore him, obey him." He was immediately enthroned as the new Satguru.

It was in June, 1971, that the boy guru first came west to England. At that time there were only a couple of hundred interested people outside his large Indian following. Since that visit, however, the growth of the mission has been phenomenal: 50,000 people have taken knowledge in the United States, 8,000 in the United Kingdom, 5,000 in Europe and 5,000 in South Africa (these figures have probably doubled since publication), and there are many more fringe members who have not yet been fully initiated. *The Chicago Tribune* (July 15, 1974) claims that "eight million followers think he's God." At present there are thirty-one headquarters in the United Kingdom.

The organization is efficiently run, each *ashram,* or temple, functioning as a commune-type dwelling for some of the devotees. There are Divine Sales (second-hand stores for making money) and a World Peace Corps (a kind of maintenance department which keeps premises and vehicles in order). Their beliefs are propagated by *satsangs,* or discourses, held in their own or hired halls or university lecture rooms. Often these meetings are blitz advertised in a very professional way. There is also a film, *Lord of the Universe,* which was first shown in University College, London, in June, 1972. This was filmed by a Swiss company at the DLM Temple in London but is now widely used by the Mission itself. The song, with the same title as the film, is also popular among devotees, and there is now an LP of DLM music which is sometimes played at meetings. Other films like

Satguru Has Come are also used, and the newspapers *Divine Times* (British) and *Divine Light* (American) are frequently sold.

The organization is very wealthy, taking in and spending an estimated three million dollars a year. The mission hit the headlines in November, 1972, when it was reported from Delhi that the Guru had been stopped by the Indian customs in his chartered jumbo jet, with a suitcase containing money, watches and jewels valued at $46,000. And the DLM was again in the headlines when it promoted an extravaganza in the Astrodome in November, 1973.

The Guru has publicly stated that he intends to spend a lot of time in the West in the future. At the time of this writing he is living in Denver, the U.S. headquarters of the DLM, and driving around in one of his Maseratis and Rolls Royces, "reserved solely for the Guru and his family."

DISTINCTIVE FEATURES *Language* The Guru has a great gift for expressing typical Hindu ideas in the language of the West. Particularly popular are Christian expressions, for example, the word, the name, baptism in the Holy Ghost, the light, the kingdom of heaven. These are all made to apply to the Hindu concept of enlightenment. The Guru feels justified in doing this since he considers, as do most Hindus, that Jesus was just another avatar like himself, who came to impart the same enlightenment or knowledge of "god." It makes communication with DLM followers very difficult, however. Often one gets the impression that they agree with what a Christian is saying, when in fact they understand quite different things by the same words. One Christian preacher was once complimented by a devotee after an address because the devotee had "seen the light of the Guru" through the Christian sermon!

One particularly awkward confusion arises over the use of the term *Christ*. For Christians this is usually taken to refer to the distinct historical person, Jesus Christ. DLM followers, however, frequently apply the title *Christ* to any and every Perfect Master there has ever been, including, of course, Maharaj Ji. This can greatly incense Christians who hear the Guru being spoken of as a reincarnation of *Christ* and assume this is a claim to identity with Jesus their Lord.

Use of Scripture Like most Hindus, the Guru accepts the Bible as authentic scripture, but since the aim of any scripture is to help one to experience "god," careful, scientific exegesis is unnecessary. He applies the prophecies of Christ's second coming to himself (for example, the phrase *coming in the clouds* is interpreted as Maharaj Ji flying into the London airport). He is fond of expounding the texts "The kingdom of heaven is within you" and "Blessed are the pure in heart, for they shall see God" with obvious Hindu interpretations. But when a careful explanation of a Bible passage which threatens Hindu ideas is attempted, DLM followers usually take refuge in the belief that ideas and words are useless; it is experience that counts.

The Way to Knowledge The Guru has no use for the chanting of *Mantras* of the conventional Hindu type and advocates instead meditating on a secret, unpronounceable mantra (also called "word" or "name," especially in DLM exegesis of biblical texts). He reveals this true mantra to the devotee in an initiation ceremony called "taking knowledge." This is an inner experience, described in terms of hearing music, seeing light and tasting nectar. It is claimed that in this experience a man is directly perceiving the oneness of the universe, which the Guru seems to identify in some quasi-scientific way with energy (the "primordial vibration"). Once the devotee has experienced this word or light he is instructed to meditate on it as often as possible and to practice devotion to the Guru by service to the local ashram. By this means he progresses to permanent and total "god"-consciousness.

There are no dietary or moral requirements, though ashrams are usually vegetarian. The Guru explicitly rejects any need for repentance. As the devotee practices meditation, he frequently seems to develop a glazed expression that has lost all sign of personality. Distinct personality, of course, is a feature of the maya and therefore the devotees see this as no loss. Such a glazed look is a sign that the person is being taken up into "god"-consciousness.

The Future The Guru occasionally makes veiled and rather mysterious prophecies about the future. His technique of meditation is especially effective, he claims, at this stage in the cycle of history—the end of the Piscean age (*raliyuga*) and the dawn of the age of Aquarius. He expects the next ten years to be very dangerous, but after that the Aquarian age will commence.

SOME TYPICAL QUOTATIONS Questions answered by Guru Maharaj Ji:
Q. Guru, can you explain where God is to be found?

A. God is in our hearts. Look into them and you will find him. How to look into them, this is the knowledge.

Q. Can I reach God through prayer, or is it just through meditation?

A. Meditation is the direct process, because speaking words is indirect. . . . But the knowledge is the perfect technique. It is the direct technique.

Q. But I've got so many things I want to say to God. I must express my feelings to him. Can't I do this in meditation?

A. No, because in meditation you have the opportunity to go to God directly. If you want to speak something to him, speak it to me, and I'll give you the answer. I'll get the answer back direct from God and speak it to you. But if you want to communicate directly with God, then meditate. Talk to him in the language of meditation. This is much holier and more perfect than these words.

Q. I want to ask questions about your validity, your genuineness.

A. You cannot ask that question. You only ask because you haven't received knowledge. . . . When you receive knowledge there will be no such questions. . . .[1]

Q. Are God and Satan the same thing?

A. God is in Satan also. God is everywhere. You know, what is God? God is this Holy Word "In the beginning was the Word and the Word was with God and the Word was God." That is the Word, that is God . . . and this Word exists everywhere, in you, in every human being.[2]

Q. How does suffering exist, do you know? . . .

A. Evil is nothing. Evil is the ignorance of our mind.

Q. The Bible, the New Testament, tells that Jesus is living now.

A. So Jesus is living, right! Jesus is living, Ram is living now, Krishna is living now, Buddha is living now, but they have all been united into one very powerful power. And when this power spreads its hand . . . all the things that are going on wrong in this world are going to be abolished.

Q. Will it be very long?

A. Very shortly. He is starting to move his hand now, you know. I want to say this to the whole world. They read the Bible and try to understand it through their minds, right? They can't understand it. Spirituality cannot be described and cannot be understood by the mind. Mind is imperfect. . . . Mind always projects what is false. Mind is a black light.

Q. Guru, why did the people kill Jesus Christ?

A. If Jesus Christ wasn't crucified nobody would have respected him. Everybody can remember Jesus Christ because he was hanging upon the cross.

Q. Are they going to respect you?

A. Yes, I'm going to be strict about it.[3]

THE HARE KRISHNA MOVEMENT (ISKCON)

Hare Krishna is a Vedantist Hindu movement of a reasonably orthodox type, employing bhakti yoga, centered around the Spiritual Master, His Grace A. C. Bhaktivedanta Swami Prabhupada. Its full title is the International Society for Krishna Consciousness.

HISTORY According to Indian tradition, Krishna appeared in India around 3,000 B.C. and taught his disciple Arjuna. This is recorded in some detail in the Bhagavad Gita. The last incarnation of Krishna, according to the ISKCON, was in A.D. 1486 in India, when Lord Caitanya appeared. He began an unbroken chain of disciplic succession which came down to His Divine Grace Sri Srimad Bhakitisiddhanta Sarasvati Gosvami Maharaja at the beginning of this century. It was from this Spiritual Master that Prabhupada, the Guru of the movement, was initiated in 1933. He was specifically ordered to spread Krishna-consciousness in the West. In 1965 (when he had reached the Hindu stage of *sannyasa,* renunciation) he came to the United States to do this. The movement first reached London in 1968. Prabhupada, now a very old man, spends his time in translating Hindu books and writing letters to his disciples. There are three temples in England now, and about thirty-five in the United States. George Harrison of the Beatles has given large amounts of money to the group.

DISTINCTIVE FEATURES *The Mantra* Great importance is attached to the chanting of mantras as a means to attaining enlightenment (Krishna-consciousness). In particular, Lord Caitanya revealed that in the kaliyuga, the best way to spiritual realization was through chanting the holy name of "god": "Hare Krishna, Hare Krishna, Krishna Krishna, Hare Hare, Hare Rama, Hare Rama, Rama Rama, Hare Hare." (Krishna and Rama are both titles of "god.") A state of ecstasy and a trance-like appearance as noted in DLM devotees is also common among chanters.

Culture The group follows a traditional ascetic Hindu cultural pattern far more closely than DLM. In addition to commune-like temple life, the true devotee dresses in a special Indian fashion and is subject to food regulations (no eggs, meat, fish, stimulants or intoxicants) and strict sexual discipline (intercourse is permitted only between married couples, once a month). Male devotees wear a *sikha* (a shaved head with hair-tuft) and carry a row of 108 beads (usually in a shoulder bag). These beads are a rosary; the Krishna mantra is chanted sixteen times on each bead every day. The robe is usually saffron in color, and disciples frequently paint their bodies and faces. All these features indicate devotion to Krishna in some way.

Publicity The group publicizes its teachings mainly by *sankirtana*, that is, by performing their chanting on city streets, and by selling their magazine, *Back to Godhead*.

The Vedic Scriptures The group is much more orthodox in the importance it gives to the Vedic scriptures than DLM, and the intellectual study of Hindu books is encouraged. After about seven years as a student and teacher with ISKCON, a disciple may attain the distinction of *swami*, but only after a searching examination in Vedic teaching. The group regards the Bible and the Koran as genuine scriptures but maintains that they have become very distorted in translation and interpretation over the centuries.

Food All food is offered to Krishna and thereby becomes spiritual (*prasadam*). Eating such food is an act of devotion and an aid to "god"-consciousness.

Other religions They claim (as do DLM and TM) to have no desire to change any man's religion, but only to make him "a better Christian" or "a better Muslim," since Krishna-consciousness is the underlying experiential truth in all religions. "The first principle of all religions is that I am not this body." In contrast to the Divine Light Mission and Transcendental Meditation, there seems to be a clear retention of the spirit-matter dichotomy in Prabhupada's philosophy. He makes no attempt to identify Krishna with the indestructible energy of modern physics.

SOME TYPICAL QUOTATIONS "The transcendental vibration established by chanting Hare Krishna is a sublime method of reviving our transcendental consciousness. As living spiritual souls, we are all originally Krishna-conscious entities; but due to our association with matter from time immemorial, our consciousness is now adulterated by our material atmosphere. The material atmosphere in which we are now living is called *maya* or illusion.... Krishna-consciousness is not an artificial imposition on the mind. This consciousness is the original natural energy of the living entity. When we hear the transcendental vibration, this consciousness is revived. This simplest method of meditation is recommended for this age.... This chanting of the Hare Krishna mantra is enacted from the spiritual platform, and thus the sound vibration surpasses all lower strata of consciousness—namely, sensual, mental and intellectual. There is no need, therefore, to understand the language of the mantra, nor is there any need for mental speculation or any intellectual adjustment.... It is automatic.... In the beginning there may not be the presence of all transcendental ecstasies. These are eight in number: (1) being stopped as dumb; (2) perspiration; (3) standing up of hairs on body; (4) dislocation of voice; (5) trembling; (6) fading of the body; (7) crying in ecstasy; (8) trance. But there is no doubt that chanting for a while takes one immediately to the spiritual platform and one shows the first symptom of this in the urge to dance along with the chanting of the mantra."[2]

"There are two kinds of activities, good and bad. If you act nicely and perform pious activities then you get good fortune, and if you act sinfully then you have to suffer.

Q. What is the duty of a person who does not believe in the scriptures?

A. His duty is to go to hell.

Q. How can it be changed for him?

A. By coming here and chanting Hare Krishna."[3]

"In this age there is no religion other than glorifying the Lord by utterance of his holy name, and that is the injunction of all the revealed scriptures. So on the order of my Spiritual Master I chant the holy name of Krishna and I am now mad after his holy name. Whenever I utter it I forget myself completely; sometimes I laugh, sometimes I cry, and sometimes I dance like a madman. I thought within myself that I may have actually gone mad by this process of chanting the holy name. . . . My Spiritual Master then informed me that it is the real effect of chanting the holy name that it produced transcendental emotion which is a rare manifestation. The transcendental emotion is the sign of the love of God which is the ultimate end of life."[4]

TRANSCENDENTAL MEDITATION

Transcendental Meditation is a yoga therapy based on the Hindu philosophy of Maharishi Mahesh Yogi.

HISTORY The Maharishi was a disciple of a reasonably important Hindu scholar, Brahmanda Sarasurati, who began a movement of spiritual regeneration in northwest India. The Maharishi himself studied physics at Allahabad University, and this is often reflected in his "scientific" approach to meditation. It was the interest of the Beatles in the sixties that first brought TM to the attention of the West. Since then the influence of the group has grown into big business, with 100,000 meditators and 4,500 teachers. There are faculties opening in the United States for the "Science of Creative Intelligence" and even the

United States army has expressed interest in the technique. In London it is represented by the Spiritual Regeneration Movement, which has about twenty other branches scattered through the British Isles.

A considerable number of scientific research papers have been published in recent years, claiming to lend support to the positive therapeutic effects of TM.[1] Dr. Peter Fenwick, a psychiatrist at Maudsley Hospital in London, has done EEG investigations on a group of meditators and believes he has observed a unique pattern of alpha and theta waves in the brain during meditation. It has also been shown recently that the metabolic rate and breath rate fall noticeably during meditation.[2]

DISTINCTIVE FEATURES *A Psychiatric Therapy* Unlike DLM and ISKCON, TM is presented to the new initiate, at least at the beginning, as just a technique for improving psychological performance. Reaction times, perceptual ability, learning ability, reduced drug dependence—evidence is presented for improvement in all these areas as a result of using TM.

Many people therefore pay their $35 to $75 fees as an investment in psychological health. In particular, the Maharishi emphasizes that TM eliminates stress, the commonest twentieth-century nervous disease. This psychiatric therapy approach, however, conceals the fact that a very clear Hindu, monistic philosophical interpretation is placed on all meditative experiences obtained.

The Technique The meditative technique taught by TM involves the silent rehearsing of a mantra under the guidance of a personal tutor. By this means, mental activity is transcended until one reaches a state of restful alertness. During meditation everything goes by itself, automatically and effortlessly. The Maharishi's name for the underlying oneness of the universe is "Creative Intelligence." It is this energy that the meditator taps when he penetrates in his meditation beyond distinguishable thought processes into the area of "pure consciousness."

Scientific The Maharishi is fond of arguments from physical science to substantiate his philosophy. The principle of least action and the laws of thermodynamics ("as activity increases, order and harmony decrease") are examples of this. Many highly lettered scholars contribute to the TM magazine *Creative Intelligence* and add to the general air of intellectual respectability which surrounds the group. Nevertheless, the Hindu roots are not far below the surface, and in the TM initiation ceremony a disciple must pay homage to the Maharishi's own Spiritual Master. There is a great danger that an agnostic who learns the TM technique will get subtly and almost unconsciously sucked into a commitment to monistic philosophy. The Maharishi also speaks of the experience of Creative Intelligence as experiencing Being itself. The links with existentialist thought (for example, Heidegger) and some contemporary Christian theology (for example, Tillich and Bultmann) is very clear here, and perhaps further explains the fascination of TM for some intellectuals.

Comparison with Other Groups Typically, there is no dogma to be believed nor any question of changing a man's religion. The teaching is as old as mankind, and universal in its application." A disciple spends only about twenty minutes each day in meditation, and this may be why there seem to be fewer signs of trance or euphoria in these meditators than in DLM and ISKCON. There seem to be no ascetic practices tied to the teachings of the Maharishi.

SOME TYPICAL QUOTATIONS "We can describe the benefits of TM in philosophical or spiritual terms. It is obeying the injunction 'know thyself' in the closest and most intimate way possible by direct experience. It fulfills the biblical command to seek the kingdom of heaven within. In practical terms it means peace of mind and relief from stress and strain."[3]

"Creativity is the cause of change and is present everywhere at all times. Intelligence is a basic quality of existence exemplified in purpose and order of change. The single and branching flow of energy (creativity) and directedness (intelligence) is called creative intelligence. The Science of Creative Intelligence arose from the major discovery that there exists in every human being this constant source of intelligence, energy and happiness. This source can be easily and systematically drawn upon by everyone for spontaneous use in everyday life, bringing personal integration and a harmoniously productive relationship with others and the world."[4]

"Maharishi's critique of consciousness is of equal interest to psychology and philosophy. His basic postulate is that existence—which conducts the

objective phase of life—and intelligence—which conducts its subjective phase—are the same at their most
fundamental level. And that during TM this integration of opposites is directly experienced.... What the
Maharishi is now offering is a subjective invariable as
a means of gaining knowledge. He says 'knowledge
gained by objective means will always be specific and
not total. The abstract unmanifest value of the pure
field of creative intelligence can never be determined
by the objective means of gaining knowledge.' "[5]

MYSTICISM: A CHRISTIAN CRITIQUE

MYSTICAL EXPERIENCES There can be no doubt that the potential for mystical experience of various kinds is part of the common heritage of the human race. It is possible to rationalize such experiences in psychological (for instance, Jungian) terms,[1] just as it is possible to rationalize Christian conversion experiences in psychological terms.[2] Such interpretations may be quite valid within their own frame of reference, but the Christian need not accept that they are a complete description or in any sense an ultimate explanation of why man is capable of such experiences. The Bible teaches us that man is made in "the image of God" and for relationship with God. It is no surprise to the Christian, then, that the human psyche has spiritual capacities which witness to this transcendental dimension of man.[3] The Christian does not need, therefore, to try to disprove or to invalidate mystical experience, nor to deny the fact that it reflects the spirituality of man. For, according to Jesus, a human being is more than matter (Mt. 4:4).

All the groups discussed in this analysis, however, have absolutized mystical experience in such a way as to make it the proper and only way of coming to know "god." This experience-based theology is open to several difficulties.

How Do You Interpret Mystical Experience? By nature, mystical experience is totally subjective and non-verbalizable. It cannot therefore be self-interpreting into theological or philosophical language: "Because the experience is inarticulate, has no sensory shape, colour or words, it lends itself to transcription in many forms, including visions of the cross or of the goddess Kali: thus a genuine mystical experience may mediate a bona-fide conversion to practically any creed, Christianity, Buddhism or Fire worship."[4]

It is a fallacy, therefore, to say that "taking the Guru's knowledge" brings its own authentication of the Guru's teaching. For the monistic philosophy of the Guru is an imposition *on to* the mystical experience, not an extraction from it. The devotee is taught to interpret his experience in accordance with Hindu philosophy. He does not learn his philosophy from his experience. He could equally well be taught quite contrary ideas about the nature of God from the same experience if he had happened to be instructed by a Mohammedan Sufi or instructed by a Roman Catholic monk.

Is Mystical Experience Really the Ultimate? We are only too aware that a man can get hooked on certain experiences and thereby miss out on true human fulfillment. Alcoholism and drug dependence are two examples. Behavior and experiences deriving from a drunken or drugged state bear marked similarity to some mystical experiences resulting from chanting or meditation. The fact that Hindu groups generally disapprove strongly of drugs and intoxicants as a means to enlightenment does not remove the worry that they may be inculcating the same kind of dependency on experiences. How does one know that, in wallowing in what he takes to be "god"-consciousness, he is not hooked on something which is in fact less than God, and that as a consequence he will miss out on real human fulfillment?

Another example of getting hooked on experience is certain kinds of eroticism. It is possible for a man to obtain erotic experience quite outside the context of its proper area of expression in the interpersonal commitment of marriage. Such eroticism may become habitual and enslaving to the destruction of the man's seeking for true fulfillment in a marital relationship. A Christian may ask if mysticism cannot be just this kind of egocentric exploitation of man's spiritual capacity rather than a proper fulfillment of it, a type of spiritual masturbation in which desires and feelings which ought to be turned outward to the distinct, personal Creator God and Father of Jesus Christ have been introverted and debased. Consequently, the potential of a man for real personal communion with God has been obscured.

Is Inner Harmony and Peace a Test of Truth? Nothing is more restful than a corpse. The fact that a man is rendered more peaceful and free from stress by mystical experience does not necessarily mean it has helped him or brought him nearer to God. It is possible to cry "Peace" when there is no peace, to soothe when we ought to warn, to be calm when we ought to fear. Psychologists and philosophers have done their best to analyze the tensions that are implicit in being a human being: ego—super-ego, rationality—feeling, etc. A peace achieved only by jettisoning one or more of these conflicting human faculties (for example, by getting rid of the super-ego and its moral inhibitions or by getting rid of rationality and its deterministic implications) is no real peace at all. Rather it is a kind of psychic leucotomy[5]—peace at the price of irrationality or amorality.

By absolutizing mystical experience, Eastern philosophy is implying that there is no ultimate significance in human reason or in the sense of moral responsibility. Rather, it says, these can be evils that hinder a man from experiencing the non-rational, non-moral cosmic-consciousness. A man's mind and his individual responsibility, then, are enemies he must excise or transcend if he is to find peace. But the Christian may ask if he has not removed his humanity in the same process. May there not be a peace and a fulfillment which makes sense of man's moral conscience and his rationality? If so, isn't the peace which mysticism offers a dangerous red herring?

In reply to these three difficulties, the Christian asserts that subjective human experience cannot be the sole ground upon which to build our knowledge of God. It is too uncertain in every way. The Christian points instead to history, and in particular to Jesus Christ, as the arena of God's personal, objective self-revelation and the proper ground for man's knowledge of God. Jesus said, "If you had known me, you would have known my Father also; henceforth you know him and have seen him" (Jn. 14:7). The apostle John wrote, "No one has ever seen God; the only Son, who is in the bosom of the Father, he has made him known" (Jn. 1:18).

Jesus called men into personal relationship with God as Father, and in the context of that relationship a man may, of course, sometimes experience deep devotion or ecstasy. Paul seems to mention such an occasion in 2 Corinthians 12:2-4, and perhaps John's experience on Patmos is another (Rev. 1:10). But, for the Christian, such mystical experiences are not the ground rock of his relationship with God. No matter how treasured such experiences of God's love and person may be, a Christian's assurance hinges on his trust in the God who has spoken in history rather than on any personal subjective experiences of his own. The story of Job is about a man who lost all sense of the nearness of God, yet remained a man of faith. "Blessed are those," said Jesus, "who have not seen and yet believe" (Jn. 20:29). Furthermore, the Bible insists that moral character is of far more importance than such subjective experiences in assessing spiritual progress (1 Cor. 13:1-3).

Most Christian mystics have always been very conscious of this: "All visions, revelations, heavenly feelings and whatever is greater than these, are not worth the least act of humility, being the fruits of that charity which neither values nor seeks itself, which thinketh well, not of self, but of others . . . many souls, to whom visions have never come, are incomparably more advanced in the way of perfection than others to whom many have been given."[6]

Christian mystics have also always emphasized the potential spiritual danger in mystical experience: "So long as the subject recognizes these mystical experiences as totally unmerited blessings and feels obligated by gratitude to produce, in as far as it lies in his power, works which are good according to their kind, they can lead him towards the light. But if he allows himself either to regard the experience as a sign of superior merit, natural or supernatural, or to idolize it as something he cannot live without, then it can only lead him into darkness and destruction."[7]

MEDITATION AND CHANTING AS DISCIPLINES

If there is such a thing as authentic, Christian, mystical experience or vision of God, it may be asked whether the techniques of Eastern mysticism, which are directed at attaining such experiences, may not properly be used by Christians. Provided we are clear about our theistic presuppositions from historical revelation, may not the techniques of Hindu meditation or chanting lead a Christian to a true experience of God's essence? Indeed, could not some Eastern mystics be really touching God or the "cosmic Christ" by such means, although they are perhaps misinterpreting their experience for lack of a Bible? Certainly some Christians today are taking Eastern-type meditation very seriously. There are, however, several pointers that ought to give us pause before we rush into mystical meditation techniques as the answer to our devotional problems.

Visions of God Are by Grace, Not by Works It is clear from the Bible that experiences that may perhaps be called "mystical" are never sought or worked for. The God of the Bible is not an impersonal ocean of energy which we may tap as and when we please. He is an omnipotent, personal Being who chooses if and when he will reveal himself to man. A prophet is always a man called and sent by God—never a man who chose and found God by his ascetic or meditative discipline. Any revelation of God, then, is a matter of grace (Mt. 11:25-27; Gal. 1:16). It is the result of God's granting a man some experience of himself, never of a man's fulfilling the right psychological or spiritual conditions to turn on the tap. Thus, such experiences always strike men in Scripture out of the blue. Examples which we may cite are Moses and the burning bush in the desert (Ex. 3:1-6), Balaam sitting on his donkey (Num. 22:31), Joshua surveying the battle (Josh. 5:13-15), Isaiah at his temple duty (Is. 6:1-13), Ezekiel by the river Chebar (Ezek. 1:1-28), Paul on the Damascus Road (Acts 9:3-9), John in his Sunday worship (Rev. 1:9-17). If a man is to give himself to meditation, it must not be for the ulterior motive of getting mystical experiences from God; for such experiences cannot be worked for.

The Example of Jesus Jesus never encouraged meditation of the Eastern type. Instead, he taught his disciples to pray (see page 14). He defined love for God in practical and moral terms (Jn. 14:23-24; 15:10), not devotional and pietistic ones. He warned men of the danger of using vain, heathen repetitions in prayer (Mt. 6:7). The prayer he taught was simple, rational and short. He does not seem to have encouraged ecstatic experience and specifically warned that such experiences were no criterion of a man's real relationship with God (Mt. 7:22). If meditation techniques of the mind-emptying or mantra-rehearsing type were positive and useful, Jesus never said so.

The Activity of Satan One of the blind spots of Eastern mysticism, when its methods are assessed in the light of the Bible, is its insensitivity to the possibility of spiritual deception. Jesus and the apostles are constantly warning about this (Mt. 7:15; 24:11; 2 Pet. 2:1; 1 Jn. 4:2-3). The Holy Spirit is not the only spiritual power in the world. Jesus had to do battle continually with one to whom he referred as the Liar (Jn. 8:44), and he warned us that we would need to use all our Christian powers of discernment if we were to identify some of his deceptions (Mt. 24:24).

Now Eastern meditation plainly lays aside precisely those critical faculties of individual cognition upon which a man relies in making value judgments. Satan is quite capable of providing spiritual experiences for the undiscerning. And there is evidence that some, if not all, of the mystic experiences obtained by using Eastern meditative techniques are being exploited by Satan in this way. We have noted several times that personality dislocation is often observed particularly among DLM and ISKCON devotees. Some psychiatrists have noted, too, a similarity between mystical experiences and the experiences of those suffering from a manic-depressive psychosis. In the Bible, personality dislocation of this kind is always interpreted spiritually in terms of the direct action of Satan. Satan's desire is to devour human personality until, like the demoniac Legion, a man just does not know who he is (Lk. 8:30). According to the Bible, and in contrast to Hindu philosophical presuppositions, human individuality is important to God and will be preserved and enhanced in his eternal kingdom. (See Mt. 13:43; 20:23; 25:23; 1 Cor. 15:35-55; 1 Thess. 5:23; 2 Tim. 4:18.)

There is, then, good reason to believe that if meditation and mantra-chanting result in loss of personality or psychological disorder, it is because Satan is involved in the experiences obtained by these means. Some Christians believe that by the chanting of heathen mantras, long associated with spiritism in India, and by the uncritical opening of the mind in meditation, mystics may be giving Satan access in some special way to their mind and personality. The possibility should at least be taken very seriously.

In summary, then, there seem to be clear grounds for treating the mind-emptying and mantra-rehearsing types of meditative technique with great caution, even where the subjects are fully aware of the fallacies of the religious syncretism of Hindu monism. What is more, there is no biblical warrant for believing that a meditator is more likely to be granted some true experience of God than any other Christian. God may meet a man in some particular experience in the context of his devotional life (Isaiah, John) or equally in the humdrum of living (Moses, Paul). A Christian, then, ought to be more concerned to be living in prayer and obedience to God's Word than to be constantly searching for mystical experiences.

THE CHALLENGE OF EASTERN THOUGHT

In previous chapters we have looked critically at mysticism in the light of biblical teaching. But our approach must not be entirely negative. There is a challenge implicit in the recent and increasing interest in Eastern thinking that plumbs very deep and important issues. Christians who wish to answer that challenge must be prepared for a tough reappraisal of their own faith. Certainly it will demand a greater concern that our religion should firmly unite heart and head. Unfortunately it is impossible in an introduction of this size to investigate the relevant questions in detail. But perhaps I can map out the central area against which the challenge is leveled, and indicate the way to the necessary, positive, Christian reply.

THE CHALLENGE TO CHRISTIAN THEOLOGY

One of the reasons why Christianity is ill-equipped to rebuff a challenge from the East at the present time is that there has been in recent years a pronounced failure of intellectual nerve in the church. The same hyper-tolerant spirit that we noted at the beginning as being characteristic of the contemporary scene has also invaded Christian thinking. Dogma is largely played down in the mainstream churches, and even among some evangelicals there is a widespread feeling that theology is a dangerous and unnecessary encumbrance. If Christians are to meet adequately the threat posed by Eastern sects, however, it is vital that we realize that the conflict is at root a *theological* one.

We indicated in the second chapter that the center of the controversy between Christianity and Eastern mysticism lies in the realm of epistemology (the philosophy of knowing) and its theological corollary, that is, how we know God. We must now look at this issue more closely.

The problem of knowledge, how we attain it, how we measure its reliability, has dominated philosophy for centuries. At present a line is usually drawn between two types of knowledge which are held to be categorically different. The first, emphasized by the *logical-empiricist* school, we may call *objective* knowledge. It comprises matters of fact which can be verified by the strict canons of logic and empirical observation. The second type of knowledge, emphasized by *existentialists*, we may call *subjective*. It embraces all those areas of human feeling and value judgment which cannot be verified in the way the empiricists demand. In ordinary speech, for instance, we may say, "I *know* that tomatoes are red" (an objective fact) but also, "I *know* fear" (a subjective feeling). The correctness of this division into objective and subjective dimensions is deeply ingrained in Western thought. It is reflected in the division of university faculties into "Sciences" (objective) and "Arts" (subjective).

Until very recently it was generally assumed that objective scientific knowledge was somehow more reliable and true than value judgments and experience. At least this was so in the West. However, as we have already repeatedly mentioned, Eastern thought diverges markedly from the West on this issue. The maya is the objective conventional world. But Eastern thought regards this objective world as essentially unreal. It gives by far the greater significance to the subjective, experiential kind of human knowledge.

Today we are witnessing an energetic reaction against the logical-empiricist type of philosophy. Science faculties cannot find students to fill their places, and existentialists are greatly influencing literature and art. It is no surprise, in this atmosphere, to find a new interest in mysticism in our culture, for there is a close epistemological link between existentialism and Eastern thought.[1] If Christians are to find a positive reply to these Eastern sects, they must become involved in the contemporary debate on the problem of knowledge.

The task is to find a solution to the objective-subjective dichotomy. It must be clear to a Christian that in at least one sphere of knowledge—the theological one of knowing God—the truth cannot lie either with the logical-empiricists or with the mystics. God cannot be worked out logically or experimented on, as if he were the object of some scientific enquiry. Yet neither can a Christian accept that God is a feeling or value judgment like fear or joy that originates within man. God does not cease to exist when I cease to know him. Nor can he be different for each man. Here is a case of human cognition which cannot be squeezed into the objective or the subjective category and seems to bridge the two.

Well-meaning theologians of the past have tried, of course, to fit God into one category or the other. The *deists* effectively made God into a kind of logical deduction. Even quite orthodox theologians of the last century tried to prove the existence of God from their observation of the universe. But such attempts to rationalize God could not result in a man's truly knowing God in the *personal* sense which the Bible describes. Others, in this century, have turned God into a feeling. Existentialist theologians tend to be indifferent to the historical veracity of the Bible because, for them, the encounter with God is essentially subjective. Whether the story that produces this sense of God is historically true is of no real importance to them. By contrast, for the early Christians the reliability of the history that created their faith was absolutely critical. "If Christ has not been raised, your faith is futile," said Paul (1 Cor. 15:17).

The existentialists have done great service to theology in drawing us back to an awareness that faith is a distinctively *human* phenomenon. The knowledge of the empiricists could equally well be gained by a computer as by a man. But the knowledge of God cannot be obtained in that way. To that extent the existentialist theologians are right. But that does not mean that God is in no sense objective. It is because God is an objective reality that the Bible presents itself as real history and not as pious myth. What is needed is an epistemology that overcomes the antagonism between fact and feeling—a bridge between West and East. Perhaps it is significant that the Bible was born in the *Middle* East.

The signs are that secular philosophers, too, are beginning to feel the need for some epistemological synthesis of empiricism and existentialism.[2] Perhaps a simple analogy will illustrate one sort of approach that is proving influential. Consider human vision. When we look at an object, as well as seeing the detail upon which our eyes have focused, we also see a large surrounding area, the so-called peripheral zone. Human knowledge seems a bit like that. Science and empiricism concentrate their gaze on the things on which our minds can focus clearly. There is a vast field of peripheral awareness, however, which cannot be tied down in scientific terms. We may call it "existential awareness," the feelings and intuitions which a computer cannot share because it is not human. But the fact that we cannot bring these perceptions into sharp focus in the same way as scientific facts does not mean they are imaginary, any more than it would be true to say central vision is more real than peripheral. Neither is it right to draw a sharp qualitative distinction between the two types of seeing. The fact is that they always go together and even overlap.

This is best exemplified, perhaps, in the human experience of recognizing a pattern (so-called gestalt perception). Consider, for instance, how we recognize another person's face in a photograph. If we were to concentrate on individual aspects on which we can focus—the eyes, the mouth—we would fail to recognize the person. Those magazine competitions where one has to match the eyes and lips of famous people prove this point. We recognize one another by a kind of combined central and peripheral vision. The same is true of reading; if one stares long enough at a word, it somehow loses its familiarity. Similarly, if one purposely defocuses one's eyes, the word gets lost in a blur. We make sense of words by combining a *look at* with a *look around* the letters.

Now an epistemology based on this kind of model stands far more chance of unifying the experience of human cognition. The two poles of objective and subjective knowledge are not mutually exclusive, but are more like the foci of the ellipse of total human awareness. They complement one another and are sometimes knotted together in a way which makes it difficult to disentangle them.

Certainly such an epistemology seems nearer to the type of knowing to which the Bible refers when it speaks of knowing God. The deists made the mistake of believing only their central cognitive vision. God thus became a mere collection of deduced attributes like the isolated features of some celebrity in a magazine competition. The mystics make the equally disastrous mistake of purposely defocusing their minds in an attempt to erase the central awareness and exploit the peripheral. It is no surprise that they cannot put their blurred experiences into words. The Bible, however, insists that we must come to God as a *person to be recognized*. Only then will we stand a chance of properly knowing him. This is what lies behind Jesus' words, "If you had known me, you would have known my Father also" (Jn. 14:7).

Knowledge of God in the Bible is neither empiricist nor mystic; it is *personal*. This is why we have constantly had to emphasize in our comparison of Christian and mystic thought the fact that God is a personal, self-conscious Being. This knowledge clearly bridges the gulf between objective and subjective. Of course persons *are* objective realities. They do not exist only in our experience of them. We encounter them through the gateway of empirical knowledge as we *see* and *hear* them. Yet, if we treat persons only as objects, we will never really know them. We may know their height and the color of their hair, but we will never experience that distinctively human knowing which we usually call a personal relationship. To enter that relationship means to be involved *subjectively* with the person in a mutual knowing and being known. It is the same, the Bible claims, with a man's knowledge of God (Jn. 10:14-15; Gal. 4:9).

For theology the whole issue crystallizes around the doctrine of *revelation*. It is perhaps here that Christians have been so very weak in recent times.

Some of the existentialist theologians have reemphasized in a quite salutary manner the importance of *subjective* illumination in the process of coming to faith. Not that this is a *new* emphasis—it was central to the reformers' doctrine of revelation.[3] The Bible speaks clearly of revelation in both its objective and its subjective dimensions—the *Word* and the *Spirit*. The previous Western preoccupation with scientific knowledge has been reflected in a general emphasis among biblical Christians on the importance of "the Word of Truth." The current swing toward subjectivity has not surprisingly been paralleled by a renewed interest in "the Spirit." But the Word and the Spirit cannot be separated. Speech cannot be parted from the breath that creates it. The Bible teaches us that the personal God is encountered through objective revelation in the empirical realm of ordinary sense perceptions. We *see* his acts and *hear* his words, as we do those of other persons. The Word of objective revelation is there in creation, in history, in Jesus Christ and, of course, in Scripture.

The Christian cannot be indifferent, therefore, to the objective veracity of the historical events and to the Scriptures which mediate God's person to man. Yet an intellectual understanding of that Word as objectively given, or even a belief in its veracity, is not enough. Knowing *about* God is not *knowing God* himself. The Word must be applied to the heart and mind subjectively by the Spirit, so that a man *recognizes the person* behind the mighty acts and words, and enters into a personal relationship with him (Mt. 11:25-27; 1 Cor. 2:6-16; 2 Cor. 3:12; 4:6).

Thus the Word without the Spirit is sterile and puzzling to man. If it produces anything, it is only intellectual Christianity like that of the deists. On the other hand, the Spirit without the Word can be no more than an incoherent mysticism that is practically indistinguishable from dangerous intuitions wrought by evil spirits. If God is truly to be known, then, the Bible insists that there must be this cooperation between external revealed truth and internal spiritual illumination. God acts in revelation within the range of both the objective and the subjective focus of human cognition. He must do so, because he is not just a fact to be believed or a feeling to be experienced, but a person to be recognized, trusted and loved.

THE CHALLENGE TO CHRISTIAN LIVING If Christians really grasp this biblical balance, it will make a vast difference to evangelism. The non-Christian who tends to think like a logical-empiricist will often argue, "Well, *prove* to me that there is a God." If caught off balance a Christian might fall into the trap of trying to do just that. Even if the Christian were successful, however, he would not have turned the non-believer into a Christian. A more helpful approach would be to try to show the agnostic that all men have firm convictions about many things which they cannot prove—human love or beauty, for example. Are these things unreal because we cannot prove them logically? In this way he may be opened up to the subjective dimension of human awareness which his empiricist presuppositions tend to devalue.

On the other hand, the mystic or existentialist non-Christian will often say, "Well, if Jesus turns you on, OK; it's true for you; but I don't need it because I've already experienced God in my own way." The trap here is that a Christian might try to convince such a non-Christian that he does need the "Jesus experience" because it is in some way superior to anything he has so far known. But again, even if the Christian were successful, there would be no conversion. To help him really, the Christian must challenge him concerning the *historical* dimension of biblical faith. He must see that it is not merely a subjective wish fulfillment, but that there is objective evidence that demands a verdict.

We do not have to deny the reality of his mystical experiences. We need only suggest that, like a man with blurred vision trying to read a message, he is not seeing the whole meaning of knowing God. To do that he must have something on which to focus his mind—and that is Jesus and the gospel. This is how Paul challenged the religious men of Athens: "What therefore you worship as *unknown*, this I proclaim to you" (Acts 17:23). He warned them of the objective reality of future judgment on the basis of the objective evidence of the resurrection of Jesus (Acts 17:31). In the same way, Christians need to draw the attention of those inclined to mysticism to the fact that there is a real world outside which they cannot escape. And that in that real world God has revealed himself to man's understanding.

Furthermore, understanding this balance between objective and subjective elements in revelation will make Christians more cautious in judging whether a person has truly become a Christian. It is not enough to get an intellectual decision or agreement with the facts of the gospel. Equally, it will not be sufficient merely to impart some spiritual experience to him. There must be an intelligent grasp of the objective Word *and* clear evidence of the inward subjective application of that truth by the Holy Spirit. So there must be *faith* and *repentance*—a change of *mind* and a change of *heart*—before we assure a person that he is a Christian. To neglect either will produce decisions and experiences galore, but very few true and enduring conversions. The new birth is accomplished by the Word (1 Pet. 1:23) and by the Spirit (Jn. 3:5) together.

But as well as influencing evangelism in a constructive way, a rediscovery of the doctrine of inward illumination will profoundly enhance our Christian devotional life. The fact that young people are turning to mysticism is a grave reflection on the poverty-stricken quality of the average church's experience of God. The emphasis on "the Word" in recent years has produced in many congregations an academic aridity in preaching and a coldness of heart in prayer meetings. However, those who are seeking a solution to this situation in a kind of Christian imitation of the mystics are, in my view, making a serious error. There is very little difference between getting spiritually excited by chanting "Hare Krishna" in an ashram and chanting "Jesus, Jesus" in a prayer meeting.

Christians can do better than trying to work up that kind of mindless ecstasy, for they have a body of revealed truth from God himself. Their God is not a feeling but a real person with a defined and reliable character. Such a God is far more exciting than mere psychic experience. To know this God truly is a privilege and a joy. We shall want to use our minds to the full, exploring his world and his Word; but it will not be enough for us just to find out more about him intellectually. We shall long that the Spirit will make real what we learn in our experience. So we shall not see just the divine attributes, but shall go beyond them to recognize his "face" (Ps. 27:7-9).

In years gone by Christians understood more clearly this balance between the Word and the Spirit; and it showed. They were not only very great theologians. They also knew their God personally. Such a man was Samuel Rutherford, professor of divinity at St. Andrews in 1647, who died under house arrest in 1661. This was his testimony: "It were a sweet and honourable death to die for the honour of that royal and princely King Jesus. His love is a mystery to the world. I would not have believed that there was so much in Christ as there is; 'Come and see' maketh Christ to be known in his excellency and glory. I wish all this nation knew how sweet his breath is; it is little to see Christ in a book as men do the world in a map; they talk of Christ by the book and the tongue, and no more; but to come nigh to Christ and have him and embrace him is another thing."[4]

The challenge of Eastern thought is well answered by a man like that. True heart-experience of God's person should result from a solid grasp of historical biblical revelation. The popularity of the Eastern sects provides a needed imperative to Christians to work toward both a deeper theology and a deeper devotional life. This is vital if we are really to meet the needs of the whole man. Those who want to accept the challenge and start that adventure can do no better, in my view, than begin by reading *Knowing God* by J. I. Packer.[5] No recent book so combines heart and head. It ought to be studied by every Christian, whether or not they have to encounter Eastern groups. In positive terms it is a far more effective Christian answer to the appeal of mysticism than this small book could ever be.

APPENDIX: PRACTICAL ADVICE TO CHRISTIANS DEALING WITH EASTERN MYSTIC GROUPS

One of the most difficult problems which the growth of Eastern mystic groups in the West brings to the Christian church is the need to communicate the gospel to people who have imbibed a totally anti-theistic philosophy. Missionaries to India have been well acquainted with the frustrations of this for years. But now, young, untrained Christians are having to face the same communication hang-up. Only a brief, personal attempt can be made here to sketch what *may* prove to be helpful lines of approach.

THINGS *NOT* **TO DO** *Do not attend Divine Light Mission and similar meetings on your own.* It is unlikely that attendance at satsang meetings or lectures will be very constructive. But if you do feel there ought to be a Christian presence, go in a group of two or three. If possible, ask some friends to pray for you while you are there. These visits have proved times of great spiritual conflict and depression for Christians in the past. I would not recommend that young Christians be taken along.

Do not swap spiritual experiences. Often Christian witness to such groups fails because it uses this approach:

"Jesus' coming into your heart is a much better experience than your Guru's knowledge."

"Taste Guru's knowledge and then you can judge."

"I don't need to, I've got Jesus."

"OK, then, when you want Guru's knowledge, you come."

It is important to distinguish *testimony* (my experience of Christ) from *evangelism* (proclamation of the historic revelation of God in Jesus Christ). By swapping experiences, Christians are playing into the hands of a mystical, experience-centered theology. Nor should you try to undermine the genuineness of the devotee's experience. You are unlikely to succeed because it probably *is* genuine.

Do not argue belligerently. Don't call the Guru anti-Christ, even if you suspect he is. Remember Paul's injunction that our speech is always to be "gracious, seasoned with salt" (Col. 4:5-6).

Do not quote isolated biblical texts. Most mystical groups can do the same, and it is often very difficult to sidestep their sophistry.

For example, suppose you quote Acts 4:12: "There is no other name under heaven given among men by which we must be saved."

"Yes!" replies the DLM devotee. "The Guru Maharaj Ji revealed that name to me."

Or, "Taste and see that the Lord is good."

"Why don't you take Guru at his word and do just that? The proof of the pudding is in the eating."

Do not get impatient when devotees do not reason carefully, or when they seem to evade your point. Remember that, as they see it, truth cannot be arrived at by intellectual pursuit, but only by experience. They get easily bored, therefore, with rational argument and, after meditating for some time, may even find rational argument difficult. Verbal reasoning, however, is the only sort of direct communication we have and so we must be patient.

SOME POSSIBLE POSITIVE APPROACHES *Treat devotees as human beings* made in the image of God, not as "specimens" of DLM or Transcendental Meditation or whatever. Let them explain their views without constantly interrupting them, and do your best to understand what they think. Don't assume that they will have a totally monistic view. Frequently Western converts to mysticism retain from their previous cultural background some feeling of God as personal and the need for prayer.

Many mysticism devotees have found a degree of social acceptance and love in their communes and ashrams which they lacked before. As Christians, we shall often need to show a more authentic spirit of love and warmth if our message is to be considered at all. Be more concerned, therefore, about the *person* than about winning the argument. If possible, talk to devotees on their own, rather than in a group.

Keep the historical Christ central to your witness. No mystic group has any clear idea of the meaning of the cross. Though they all accept Jesus as a genuine avatar, the story of his cross and resurrection are irrelevant to them, since an avatar comes to teach and to reveal "god"-consciousness. A useful conversation can sometimes begin, therefore, with the question, "Why did Jesus insist that it was necessary for him to die?" It is very easy to prove from the Gospels that this was Jesus' conviction. (See, for instance, Mt. 16:21; 17:22-23; Lk. 22:37; 24:44-47.) A devotee will usually express ignorance on this point, and the door is opened to a careful explanation of the unique atoning work which Christ came to do.

A similar approach can be made from the importance given in the Bible to the resurrection. For example, you might raise questions such as these: "If Jesus came only to give the same experience of light as your Guru, why were the disciples so shocked when he died? Why was it so important to them that he physically rose from the dead? After all, Buddha is dead, Muhammad is dead, Krishna (as an incarnation) is dead physically, Lord Caitanya is dead and one day your Guru will die. You may then be sad. But there is no reason for him to rise again because you have his light now. So why was the resurrection so important to the disciples of Jesus?"

Or again, "If Paul attained 'god'-consciousness when he saw the light on the Damascus Road, why was it so important to him later that Jesus had physically risen from the dead (1 Cor. 15:17)?"

A discussion of these points will inevitably lead to the problem of sin, and here it is important to make clear that sin and guilt are objective realities in the Bible requiring *objective* cleansing (in atonement). For a mystic, sin and guilt are *subjective* functions of one's own psyche—just the illusions of one's own ignorance and mind. We may need to awaken the conscience of our friend by speaking of the *objective* reality of judgment of which Jesus spoke. (See, for instance, Mt. 13:40-43; 24:29-51; Lk. 16:19-31.)

Question the validity of the devotee's interpretation of his experience. You are unlikely to impugn the devotee's confidence that he has had the most marvelous, mind-bending experience of his life. But you may make him ask on what basis he identifies what he has experienced with "god." If persistently challenged along this line, some devotees will agree that they were *taught verbally* the interpretation they place on their experience and that it is not self-evident from the experience itself that they are touching "god." Some of the points made on pages 35-40 are relevant here. We may ask, for example, "How does feeling peace and love prove it's true?" or "How do you know there isn't a bigger God beyond the one you've touched through the Guru?" Remember Paul's words at Athens: "What therefore you worship as *unknown*, this I proclaim to you" (Acts 17:23).

Challenge them by showing them that they are running away from the real world and its problems into mystical experience. The psychological motive a man has for any belief he holds cannot logically be held to discredit the belief itself. But it may force a man to look for deeper, objective reasons for his confidence beyond the subjective satisfaction his beliefs give him personally. Quite a few DLM and Krishna-consciousness followers are dropouts who were previously mixed up with drugs. It is fair to ask what makes them sure they won't eventually get bored with the Guru's kicks. Be careful, however! Some of these mystic devotees are rather inadequate people (this is generally true of TM), so gentleness of manner is important here if we are not to hurt or alienate them.

Warn of the danger of spiritual deception. Ask if they have observed the fixed ecstatic expressions of those who have been meditating a long while. Do they find it worrying? Why does it happen?

Pointing to verses like Matthew 7:15-20 may be useful. But the reply is frequently, "Yes, I've tried the fruits of the Guru and they are sweet!" Some discussion of the *nature* of the fruits of spirituality may be required then, and the normal answer of the Bible (that is, moral character: Jn. 15; Gal. 5:22) may not prove very clear-cut.

Similarly Matthew 24:23-27 *may* be useful. But a devotee who is familiar with the Guru's techniques in exegesis will say, "Yes, from the East to the West—just as Guru Maharaj Ji has come!" A comparison of Galatians 1:6-9 and 1 Corinthians 15:1-7, pointing out that Paul's gospel was historical and anything else was "accursed," may prove more to the point if there is time for a fairly careful Bible study.

I have found, however, that merely warning of the

reality of the devil and the danger of playing with spiritual phenomena when one has no idea of how to discriminate between good and evil, has shaken some young devotees in their self-confidence. We have a responsibility to point out that no error is harmless and that, if real spirit forces are being invoked in these mystic practices, then there is danger for all concerned.

NOTES

Introduction
[1]Richard Bach, *Jonathan Livingston Seagull* (New York: Macmillan, 1970).

Chapter 2
[1]*Divine Light*, May 1972. [2]*Divine Light*, February 1972. [3]*Divine Light*, January 1972.

Chapter 3
[1]In accordance with the group's great reverence for the Hindu scriptures, the word Krishna is usually written in a technically more correct transliteration without vowels—KRSNA. [2]From *On Chanting Hare Krishna* by Prabhupada. [3]From *Back to Godhead*, No. 35. [4]A saying of Lord Caitanya, quoted in *On Chanting Hare Krishna*.

Chapter 4
[1]See, for example, *The Scientific American*, February 1972. [2]*The Lancet*, April 1973. [3]*Transcendental Meditation: An Outline.* [4]*The Science of Creative Intelligence: A Short Introduction.* [5]*The Guardian* report, January 19, 1973.

Chapter 5
[1]Robert C. Zaehner, *Mysticism, Sacred and Profane* (New York: Oxford Univ. Press, 1961). Information supplied by Robert Cook in a private communication. [2]William Sargent, *Battle for the Mind* (New York: Harper & Row, 1972). [3]J. N. D. Anderson, *Christianity and Comparative Religion* (Downers Grove, Ill.: InterVarsity Press, 1970). [4]Arthur Koestler, *The Invisible Writing* (New York: Macmillan, 1954). [5]I am indebted to Robert Cook for this expression. [6]St. John of the Cross, quoted in Fremantle, Anne, ed., *The Protestant Mystics* (Boston: Little, Brown, 1964), pp. 31-32. [7]W. H. Auden, quoted in Fremantle, *The Protestant Mystics*, p. 13.

Chapter 6
[1]See Lit-sen Chang, *Zen-Existentialism* (Philadelphia: Presbyterian and Reformed Publishing Co., 1969). [2]See, for example, Michael Polanyi, *Personal Knowledge* (Chicago: Univ. of Chicago Press, 1958), and *The Tacit Dimension* (New York: Doubleday, 1967). [3]See, for example, John Owen, *Collected Works* (London: Banner of Truth, 1967), IV, 1-234. [4]Samuel Rutherford, *The Letters of Samuel Rutherford* (Attic Press, 1973). [5]J. I. Packer, *Knowing God* (Downers Grove, Ill.: InterVarsity Press, 1973).